HIND: L ³⁄₁₆"–⁷⁄₁₆"; W ³⁄₁₆"–⁵⁄₁₆"

Our smallest mammals. Tiny
tracks rarely show any detail.
Use tiny trail patterns to help identify.
Front and hind tracks similar in size.

Moles

FRONT: L ³⁄₈"–⁵⁄₈"; W ³⁄₁₆"–⁵⁄₈"
HIND: L ¼"–½"; W ¼"–½"

Tracks of this fossorial mammal are rarely seen.
Digging signs are quite obvious.

Harvest Mice

FRONT: L ¼"–³⁄₈"; W ¼"–⁵⁄₁₆"
HIND: L ¼"–½"; W ³⁄₁₆"–⁵⁄₁₆"

Our smallest mouse. The "thumb"
on the hind foot is set farther back
than in other mice.

House Mouse

FRONT: L ¼"–½"; W ³⁄₁₆"–³⁄₈"
HIND: L ⁵⁄₁₆"–¾"; W ⁵⁄₁₆"–⁷⁄₁₆"

Common in and around
buildings. Toes are longer and
less bulbous than white-footed mice.
Hind track are larger than front.

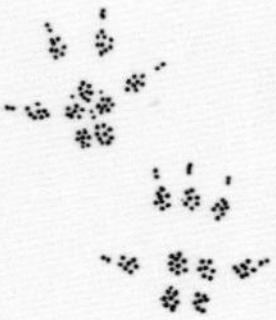

Tiny Mammals

White-footed Mice

FRONT: L ¼"–½"; W ⁵⁄₁₆"–½"
HIND: L ¼"–⁹⁄₁₆"; W ⁵⁄₁₆"–½"

Very common. Bulbous toe pads. Trail patterns resemble that of a miniature squirrel.

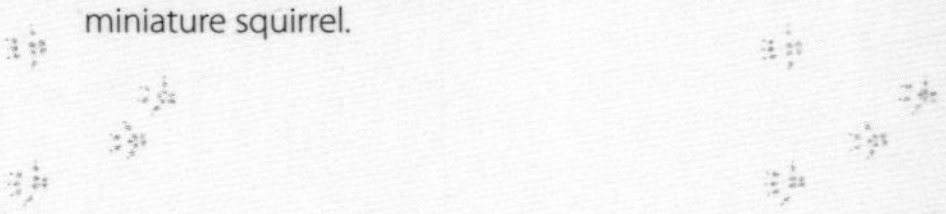

Voles & Lemmings

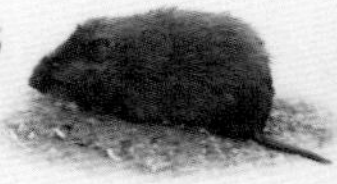

FRONT: L ¼"–½"; W ¼"–½"
HIND: L ¼"–⅝"; W ¼"–½"

Common around fresh vegetation. Long, fingery toes. Frequently walk or trot rather than bound.

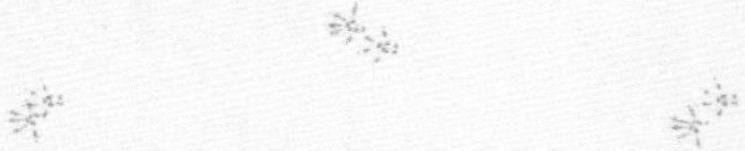

Jumping Mice

FRONT: L ⅜"–⅝"; W ⅜"–⅝"
HIND: L ½"–1⅛"; W ⅜"–¾"

Has extremely long, slender toes. May make very long leaps. Hibernates through the winter in colder climates. Hind track much larger than front.

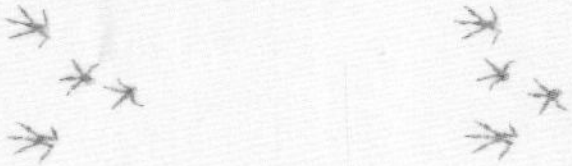

Hispid Cotton Rat

FRONT: L ⅜"–⅝"; W ⅜"–½"
HIND: L ½"–⅞"; W ½"–⅝"

Tracks are larger than those of mice but smaller than those of other rats. Found in grassy habitats. Hind track larger than front.

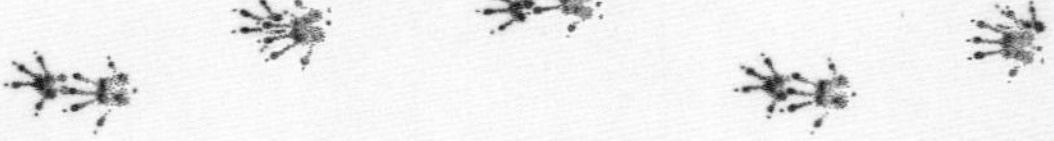

Marsh Rice Rat

FRONT: L ½"–¾"; W ½"–⅝"
HIND: L ¹¹⁄₁₆"–1¼"; W ⁹⁄₁₆"–¾"

Has long, slender toes; small pads; and narrow palms. Found in wet habitats. Hind track larger than front.

Black Rat

FRONT: L ⁷⁄₁₆"–¾"; W ½"–¾"
HIND: L ½"–1"; W ¹¹⁄₁₆"–⅞"

Toe pads are more bulbous than those of Norway rats and rice rats, less bulbous than those of woodrats. Hind track larger than front.

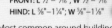

Norway Rat

FRONT: L ½"–¹³⁄₁₆"; W ½"–¹³⁄₁₆"
HIND: L ⅝"–1¼"; W ⅝"–1⅛"

Most common around buildings. Very similar to Rice Rat tracks. Use habitat and behavior to distinguish. Hind track larger than front.

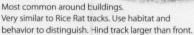

Woodrats

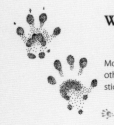

FRONT: L ⅜"–⅞"; W ⅜"–¾"
HIND: L ½"–1¼"; W ½"–⅞"

More bulbous toe pads than other rats. Builds enormous stick nests.

Eastern Chipmunk

FRONT: L ½"–⅞"; W ⅜"–¾"
HIND: L ½"–1"; W ½"–⅞"

Tracks and trails are similar to those of tree squirrels, but in miniature. Toes tend to splay less than in similarly sized rat tracks.

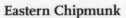

Flying Squirrel

FRONT: L ⅜"–¾"; W ⅜"–¾"
HIND: L ½"–1⅜"; W ⅜"–⅞"

Comes to the ground less often than other squirrels. Wide-set front feet create "boxy" trail patterns. Tracks and trails resemble those of chipmunks.

Red Squirrel

FRONT: L ⅞"–1¼"; W ½"–1"
HIND: L 1"–2"; W ¾"–1¼"

Long, slender toes make tracks appear more delicate than other squirrel tracks. Larger tracks than flying squirrels and smaller than those of tree squirrels.

Tree Squirrels

FRONT: L 1"–1¾"; W ½"–1½"
HIND: L 1"–2¾"; W ⅞"–1¾"

These familiar animals leave abundant tracks. Long toes and clearly defined pads distinguish them from rabbit tracks. Trails usually begin and end at trees.

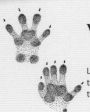

Woodchuck

FRONT: L 1⅜"–2½"; **W** 1⅛"–1⅞"
HIND: L 1⅝"–2¾"; **W** 1¼"–1⅞"

Large, stubby, squirrel-like tracks. Typically walks rather than bounds.

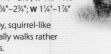

Muskrat

FRONT: L 1"–1½"; **W** 1"–1½"
HIND: L 1½"–2½"; **W** 1⅜"–2¼"

Usually found near water. Prominent claws. Long hind toes are fringed with stiff hairs.

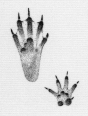

Nutria

FRONT: L 1"–2⅜"; **W** 1⅛"–2¼"
HIND: L 2⅛"–4½"; **W** 2"–3"

Non-native aquatic rodent. Tracks are similar to a beaver's, but smaller.

American Beaver

FRONT: L 2"–3½"; **W** 1½"–3"
HIND: L 4½"–7"; **W** 3"–5"

Clear hind prints are unmistakable. Trails usually lead to or from water.

Cottontail Rabbits

FRONT: L ⅞"–1¾"; W ⅝"–1¼"
HIND: L 1¼"–3¼"; W ¾"–1⅝"

Very common. Egg-shaped tracks. Distinctive triangular-shaped bounding trail pattern. Marsh rabbits and swamp rabbits walk frequently.

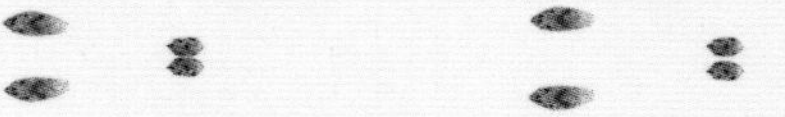

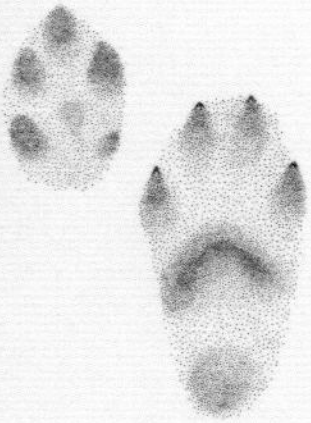

Snowshoe Hare

FRONT: L 1¾"–3"; W 1¼"–2¼"
HIND: L 3"–5"; W 1½"–4½"

Tracks and trails similar to a cottontail's, but feet are much larger. Hind feet may splay widely. Found high in the Appalachian Mountains.

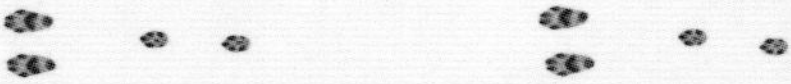

Eastern Spotted Skunk

FRONT: L 1"–1⅜"; W ¾"–1"
HIND: L ¾"–1¼"; W ⅝"–1⅛"

Tracks have a clean, compact look. Prominent claws. Irregular gaits.

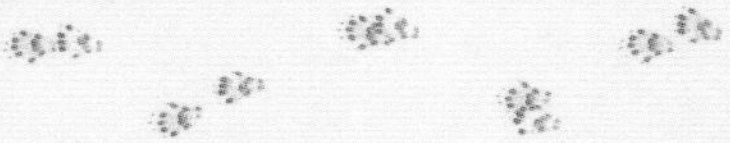

Striped Skunks

FRONT: L ⅞"–1¾"; W ⅞"–1¼"
HIND: L 1"–1¾"; W ⅞"–1¼"

Prominent claws. Toes never splay. Trails resemble those of a miniature bear.

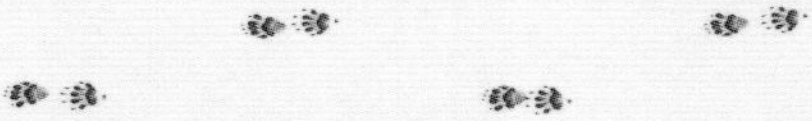

Weasels

FRONT: L ⁵⁄₁₆"–½"; W ⁵⁄₁₆"–½"
HIND: L ⁵⁄₁₆"–½"; W ⁵⁄₁₆"–½"

Our smallest carnivores. Small tracks usually arranged in a 2x2 bound pattern with highly variable strides.

American Mink

FRONT: L 1"–1¾"; W ¾"–1⅝"
HIND: L ¾"–1½"; W ⅞"–1⅝"

Usually found close to water. Individual tracks may resemble those of tree squirrels, but track patterns are usually distinctive.

Fisher

FRONT: L 2⅛"–3½"; W 2"–3¼"
HIND: L 2"–3"; W 1¾"–3"

Front tracks larger than hind. Large negative space and slender palm help distinguish from canines and felines. Found high in the Appalachian Mountains.

River Otter

FRONT: L 2"–3"; W 1⅞"–3"
HIND: L 2¼"–3¾"; W 2⅛"–3½"

Usually found near water. Typically travels in a 3x4 lope. Trails may include slides.

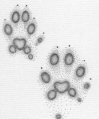

Virginia Opossum

FRONT: L 1¼"–2⅛"; **W** 1½"–2¼"
HIND: L 1½"–2½"; **W** 1½"–2⅝"

Front track has starlike shape. Hind track resembles a human hand. Tracks often overlap, creating a jumble of pads.

Ringtail

FRONT: L 1"–1½"; **W** 1"–1⅜"
HIND: L 1"–1½"; **W** ⅞"–1¼"

Tracks resemble those of house cats but have a larger palm pad. Claws rarely register. Found in AR, LA, and eastern TX.

Northern Raccoon

FRONT: L 1¾"–2¾"; **W** 1½"–2¾"
HIND: L 2"–2¾"; **W** 1½"–2¾"

Highly variable tracks often resemble human handprints. Sometimes mistaken for otter tracks, but distinctive 2x2 walking gait is diagnostic.

Black Bear

FRONT: L 3½"–6"; **W** 3½"–5½"
HIND: L 5"–8"; **W** 3½"–5¾"

Five toes and robust palm pads. Very large. Clear prints are unmistakable. Typical gait is an overstep walk with the front feet turned in.

Domestic Dog

Range from smaller than gray fox to larger than wolf or panther

Ubiquitous. Various breeds. Tracks range from coyote-like to nearly round. Stout claws often prominent, but trimmed nails may not show at all.

Gray Fox

FRONT: L 1¼"–1¾"; W 1¼"–1¾"
HIND: L 1⅛"–1¾"; W 1"–1⅝"

Our smallest wild canine. Tracks appear rounder and more "cat like" than the red fox's. Semi-retractable claws may not register.

Red Fox

FRONT: L 1¾"–2½"; W 1½"–2⅛"
HIND: L 1½"–2½"; W 1¼"–1⅞"

Heavy fur often makes features more distinct than those of other canines. Thin "bar" may show in the palm, especially in the front track.

Coyote

FRONT: L 2"–3"; W 1½"–2¾"
HIND: L 2"–3"; W 1⅜"–2¼"

Compared to domestic dogs, toes tend to register deeper than the palm; the slender claws typically point straight ahead.

Red Wolf

FRONT: L 2⅞"–3½"; W 2¼"–2¾"
HIND: L 2¾"–3¼"; W 1⅞"–2½"

Similar to coyote tracks but larger and with stouter claws. Critically endangered. Only known population is on Albemarle Peninsula in eastern NC.

House Cat
FRONT: L 1"–1⅝"; W 1"–1¾"
HIND: L 1⅛"–1⅝"; W ⅞"–1⅜"

Tracks are round with a large palm pad. Front and hind track more similar than in bobcats. Claws rarely show.

Bobcat
FRONT: L 1½"–2½"; W 1½"–2½"
HIND: L 1½"–2½"; W 1¼"–2¼"

Asymmetrical front track may be wider than it is long. Hind track is narrower, more symmetrical, and has a taller negative space.

Florida Panther
FRONT: L 2¾"–3¾"; W 2¾"–3½"
HIND: L 2½"–3¾"; W 2¼"–3¼"

Typical feline track with a large palm pad and oval to tear-drop-shaped toes. Highly endangered. Found in southern FL.

Nine-banded Armadillo
FRONT: L 1½"–2"; W 1"–1¾"
HIND: L 2"–3"; W 1½"–2¼"

Distinctive tracks have a hooflike or birdlike appearance.

Cats/Armadillo

Wild Boar
FRONT: L 2"–2½"; **W** 2⅛"–2¾"
HIND: L 1¾"–2¼"; **W** 1¾"–2¼"

Leaves prominent signs when rooting for food. Turns up earth and does considerable damage to vegetation.

White-tailed Deer
FRONT: L 2"–3½"; **W** 1⅝"–2¾"
HIND: L 1⅞"–3¼"; **W** 1½"–2½"

Extremely abundant. Distinctive and familiar heart-shaped track.

Horse
FRONT: L 4¾"–5½"; **W** 4¼"–5¼"
HIND: L 4½"–5¼"; **W** 4"–4¾"

Large, round, single-toed tracks are unmistakable.

Domestic Cow
FRONT: L 2½"–4¾"; **W** 2¼"–5¾"
HIND: L 2½"–4¾"; **W** 2¼"–4¾"

Large, rounded, two-toed tracks are unmistakable in our region. Graze on some Forest Service and Park Service lands.

American Robin
L 1¾"–2⅛"; **W** ¾"–1"

Curved toes give tracks a
"peeling banana" shape.
Large pad on the hallux.
Runs and skips, with frequent stops.

Mourning Dove
L 1⅜"–1⅞"; **W** 1"–1¼"

Squat, wide tracks. Outer toe is
straight; other toes curve inward.
Walks with short steps.

American Crow
L 2¾"–3½"; **W** 1⅛"–1⅝"

Large classic bird track with
somewhat bulbous toes. Central
and innermost toes are nearly
parallel. Walks, hops, and skips.

Bald Eagle
L 6"–7½"; **W** 3¼"–5"

Extremely large classic bird track
with robust, bulbous toes and
prominent claws. Walks.

Great Blue Heron
L 6"–8½"; **W** 4"–6"

Largest bird track in the
Southeast. Long toes are
smooth and narrow. Walks.

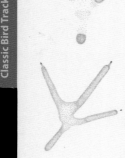

Northern Flicker

L 1¾"–2½"; W ⅜"–⅝"

Narrow K-shaped tracks. Often forages on the ground for ants. Hops.

Spotted Sandpiper

L ⅞"–1¼"; W 1⅛"–1⅜"

Symmetrical tracks with smooth, slender toes. Hallux often registers as a small "spot" behind the palm. Walks.

Wild Turkey

L 3⅜"–5"; W 3⅝"–5¼"

Large game bird track with bulbous toes and blunt nails. Palm and hallux usually register. Partial webbing at the base of toes is sometimes visible. Walks.

Ring-billed Gull

L 1⅞"–2¼"; W 2"–2⅜"

Outer toes strongly curved. Webbing usually visible. Hallux is smaller than in duck tracks and rarely registers. Palm registers about half the time. Walks.

Canada Goose

L 3¾"–4½"; W 3¼"–5"

Outer toes are curved, unlike a turkey's. Webbing usually visible. Small hallux rarely shows. Duck tracks are similar but tend to show the hallux. Walks.

Eastern Newt

FRONT: L ⁵⁄₁₆"–³⁄₈"; W ³⁄₁₆"–⁵⁄₁₆"
HIND: L ⁵⁄₁₆"–³⁄₈"; W ³⁄₁₆"–³⁄₈"

Greatly reduced outer toes give these tracks a distinctive "trident" shape, unique among salamanders of the Southeast.

American Bullfrog

FRONT: L 2"–2¾"; W ⅞"–1¼"
HIND: L 2¼"–3⅞"; W 1"–2½"

Our largest frog. Leaves complete tracks more often than smaller frogs and toads. Usually found within one bound length of the water's edge.

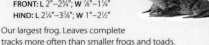

Green Anole

FRONT: L ⁵⁄₁₆"–½"; W ³⁄₁₆"–³⁄₈"
HIND: L ⅝"–¹³⁄₁₆"; W ³⁄₁₆"–½"

A highly visible lizard common in and around homes in much of the Southeast. Look for tracks in dust or sand under lush, shady vegetation.

Common Snapping Turtle

FRONT: L 1¼"–1¾"; W 1½"–2⅝"
HIND: L 1½"–2¾"; W 1½"–2"

Front feet register turned in and narrower than the hind feet, which face straight ahead. Unlike other turtles, often shows a tail drag, but not shell drag.

American Alligator

FRONT: L 3¾"–5"; W 3½"–4"
HIND: L 6"–8"; W 4"–5¼"

Among the largest tracks in the Southeast. Beavers can leave similar-looking tracks but with much smaller trails.

Individual Track Identification

If possible, locate both front and hind tracks of the animal. Then use these four steps to help identify the tracks:

1. Study the overall shape of the track.
2. Count the number of toes.
3. Look at the claw marks.
4. Measure the size of the track.

STEP 1. STUDY THE OVERALL SHAPE OF THE TRACK.

Is the track circular, oval, or lopsided? Is it wider at the front or wider at the back? Are the toes symmetrically or asymmetrically arranged?

STEP 2. COUNT THE NUMBER OF TOES.

Be careful—a lot can confound this seemingly simple task. Toes may not register clearly, or be set far off to the side. Stray marks may look like toes. Try to find multiple prints to verify your count.

STEP 3. LOOK AT THE CLAW MARKS.

Some animals have long stout claws, while others have short fine claws. Cats have retractable claws, which often do not show in their tracks at all.

STEP 4. MEASURE THE SIZE OF THE TRACK.

Measure the track's length and width. While animal foot sizes can vary tremendously within a species, track size will help you narrow down the possibilities.

HOW TO MEASURE TRACKS

Measure tracks along their longest and widest points. Measure length from the rear edge of the rearmost pad to the front edge of the foremost toe. Measure width across the widest part of the foot, including all of the toes. Look for clear tracks relatively free from distortion. If you can, measure several tracks to get an average. The measurements of mammal tracks in this guide do not include claws, except where they are indistinguishable from the toes. Measurements for bird and herp (reptiles and amphibians) tracks do include claws. Measurements for "game" and "webbed" bird tracks do not include the hallux (the rear-facing toe).

Gaits & Track Patterns

Gaits describe how an animal moves. Track patterns are the arrangement of footprints left by a particular gait. Most mammals and herps in the Southeast move on all fours, while birds walk on two legs, like us. Two-legged, or bipedal, and four-legged, or quadrupedal, gaits can each be divided into two broad categories: symmetric and asymmetric. Symmetric gaits have an even rhythm and produce lines of evenly spaced tracks or track pairs. Asymmetric gaits have an uneven rhythm, resulting in groups of tracks separated by distinct gaps.

BIPEDAL GAITS & TRACK PATTERNS

A symmetric bipedal gait is called a **walk** when the animal always has at least one foot on the ground. It is called a **run** if there is a moment when both feet are off the ground mid-stride. Both gaits produce a zigzagging line of tracks, with walks usually showing shorter steps and a wider trail than runs. Larger birds and those that spend lots of time on the ground usually walk or run.

Turkey walk

An asymmetric bipedal gait is called a **hop** when the animal jumps with both feet together, leaving side-by-side tracks. It's called a **skip** when the footfalls are staggered, resulting in offset pairs of tracks. Smaller perching birds typically hop or skip.

Crow skip

QUADRUPEDAL GAITS & TRACK PATTERNS

A quadrupedal **walk** is a symmetric gait in which the animal always has at least one front foot and one hind foot on the ground. With each step, the animal may place its hind foot on the ground either behind its front track (understep), on top of it (direct register), or in front of it (overstep). Raccoons use an extreme overstep, placing their hind foot next to the front track on the opposite side of the body. Walking is the most common gait for large rodents, "five-toed walkers," cats, deer, and most herps.

Coyote walk

A **trot** is the quadrupedal version of the bipedal run. The two legs diagonally opposite each other move at the same time, and there is a moment when the animal has all four feet off the ground. Similar to walks, trots can leave either direct register or overstep patterns. Overstep trots generally require the animal to turn its body slightly, allowing the hind feet to pass to the side of the front feet. Trots are the most common gaits for some tiny mammals, most dogs, and some lizards.

Fox trot

Lopes and Gallops are asymmetric gaits in which all four legs alternately gather and extend, creating distinct groupings of four tracks. In lopes and gallops, each foot moves independently. If the track pattern shows at least one hind foot landing even with or behind either front foot, it is generally called a lope. If both hind feet register ahead of both front feet in the group, it is generally called a gallop. Lopes are common gaits for skunks and larger weasels. Gallops are the fastest gaits used by most large carnivores and hoofed animals.

Skunk lope

Red Fox gallop

Hops and Bounds are similar to lopes and gallops, except the hind feet push off and land together. The resulting track patterns show hind tracks side-by-side, or nearly so. If the hind tracks register behind or partly behind the fronts, trackers call the gait a hop. Otherwise we call it a bound. Bounding animals' hind feet usually straddle their front feet, causing hind tracks to register wider. Smaller weasels use a modified "2x2 bound" in which their hind feet land directly in the front tracks. Hops and bounds usually produce more compact track groups than lopes and gallops, with larger spaces between groups. They are the most common gaits for frogs, many tiny mammals, squirrels, and rabbits. Many mammals bound when moving over rough terrain and use the "2x2 bound" in deep snow.

Squirrel bound

Red Fox hop

BIRD TRACK GROUPS

Most bird tracks in the Southeast fall into four categories, based on their overall shape.

Classic: Perching birds, diurnal raptors, and herons leave **classic** bird tracks showing three forward-facing toes and one similarly sized rear-facing toe, called the hallux. This is the most common bird track shape. Larger birds that leave classic tracks typically walk. Smaller species variously walk, run, skip and hop.

Zygodactyl: Woodpecker, owl, roadrunner, and parrot tracks have two toes pointing forward and two pointing backward. This track shape is called **zygodactyl**, meaning "paired toes." Woodpeckers typically hop. Owls walk.

Game: Upland game birds and wading shorebirds leave **game** bird tracks with three straight, forward-facing toes. A small hallux shows in some species. Game birds and shorebirds walk or run almost exclusively.

Webbed: Seabirds and waterfowl leave **webbed** tracks with three forward-facing toes and sometimes a small hallux. The outer toes in webbed tracks curve inward. Most waterfowl walk with their feet turned inward (oddly, the opposite of what we call "duck footed").

REPTILE AND AMPHIBIAN TRACK GROUPS

Reptiles and amphibians, or herps, have different leg structures than mammals, leading them to shift side-to-side as they move, often twisting their feet and blurring their tracks. Because of this, and their habitats, clear tracks are less common than in birds or mammals. Herp tracks are difficult to identify beyond the order, but that's often enough.

Frogs & Toads frequently hop with their front feet facing in toward each other and their much larger hind feet registering wider, slightly farther back, and angled outward. On firm substrate, often only the tips of the toes of the hind feet register, forming a pair of "check marks." Toads have shorter, stouter toes than frogs and often walk as well as hop.

Salamanders & Newts walk on land, leaving small trails of closely spaced tracks surrounding a prominent body or tail drag. Most species have four clawless toes on their front feet and five on their larger hind feet, though some toes may be very small.

Lizards typically walk, trot, or bound, leaving trails similar to those of comparably sized mammals but usually less distinct. Tracks typically show five long, slender toes on each foot tipped with sharp claws. Many trails also include some trail drag.

Bullsnake track

Snakes, which are closely related to lizards, leave distinctive serpentine body marks without accompanying footprints.

Turtles & Tortoises walk exclusively, leaving wide trails with short steps. Tracks tend to be round or wider than long, and show prominent claw marks. They have five toes on each foot, but the outermost toe on the hind foot is reduced in many species and may not register.

Crocodilians usually walk leaving a wide trail of closely spaced tracks with a tail drag down the center. They are also capable of trotting and even galloping and can move with astonishing speed. They have five toes on their front feet and four on their hind. They have claws on the first three toes of each foot but not on the outer toes.

Track Group	STEP 1: Overall Shape	STEP 2: # of Toes	STEP 3: Claws Show?	
TINY MAMMALS	Tracks generally well under 1"	4 (rodents) or 5 (others) front; 5 hind	Usually tiny dots. May be difficult to see	
SQUIRRELS	Long toes and a triangular-shaped palm	4 front; 5 hind	Fine. Usually register	
LARGE RODENTS	Long toes; hind tracks usually larger than front	4 front; 5 hind	Stout. May be indistinct from toes	
RABBITS	Egg-shaped; pads usually indistinct	5 front; 4 hind	Short, blunt. Often obscured by fur	
SKUNKS	Compact; stubby toes rarely splay	5 front & hind	Long and stout. Usually very prominent	
WEASELS	Large negative space between small toes and a chevron-shaped palm	5 front & hind	Fine. Usually visible	
FIVE-TOE WALKERS	Often resemble human hand- or footprints	5 front & hind	Variable. May or may not show clearly	
DOGS	Oval, symmetrical. Large toes make up most of the track	4 front & hind	Usually register, but can be inconspicuous	
CATS	Round, asymmetrical fronts. Large palm makes up most of the track	4 front & hind	Sharp. Usually retracted, but can be prominent	
ARMADILLO	Unique birdlike tracks; outer toes rarely register	4 front; 5 hind	Stout, prominent, but indistinct from toes	
UNGULATES	Round or heart-shaped hoof prints	1 (horses); 2 (others)	Dewclaws show at speed or in deep substrate	

Track Group Chart

Track Group	STEP 1: Arrangement of Toes	STEP 2: Shape of Toes	STEP 3: Webbing?	
CLASSIC BIRD	3 toes forward 1 toe back	Straight or curved	Sometimes at the base of the toes	
ZYGODAC-TYL BIRD	2 toes forward 2 toes back	Straight	None	
GAME BIRD	3 toes forward 0 or 1 smaller toe back	Straight	Sometimes at the base of the toes	
WEBBED BIRD	3 toes forward 0 or 1 smaller toe back	Outer toes curved	Yes, but may not register clearly	

Track Group	STEP 1: Overall Shape	STEP 2: # of Toes	STEP 3: Claws?	
FROGS & TOADS	Hind feet usually register as a pair of "checkmarks"	4 front; 5 hind	None, but toe tips resemble claw marks	
SALAMAN-DERS & NEWTS	Small, closely spaced tracks	4 front; 5 hind	None	
LIZARDS	Small. Long toes, but tracks usually indistinct	5 front; 5 hind	Typically slender. Often indistinct in tracks	
SNAKES	Serpentine body marks without footprints	None	None	
TURTLES & TORTOISES	Round to oval. May be wider than long	5 front; 5 hind (often only 4 register)	Long and stout. Often only claws register	
CROCODIL-IANS	Large tracks with long, stout toes	5 front; 4 hind	Stout claws on the 3 inner toes	

Adventure Quick Guides

Only Southern Animal Tracks

Organized by group for quick and easy identification

Simple and convenient—narrow your choices by group, and view just a few tracks at a time

- Pocket-size format—easier than laminated foldouts

- Realistic track illustrations with size information

- More than 70 mammal species—plus major groups of birds, reptiles, and amphibians

- Step-by-step guide to track identification

- Track information chart and sample gait patterns

Play your favorite games and improve your identification skills with regional playing cards

ADVENTURE
PUBLICATIONS
an imprint of Adventure**KEEN**

NATURE / ANIMALS / SOUTHEAST / GULF

ISBN 978-1-59193-949-8   U.S. $9.95